Serena Williams
Tennis

by Kate Moening

BLASTOFF!
2
READERS

BELLWETHER MEDIA • MINNEAPOLIS, MN

Note to Librarians, Teachers, and Parents:

Blastoff! Readers are carefully developed by literacy experts and combine standards-based content with developmentally appropriate text.

Level 1 provides the most support through repetition of high-frequency words, light text, predictable sentence patterns, and strong visual support.

Level 2 offers early readers a bit more challenge through varied simple sentences, increased text load, and less repetition of high-frequency words.

Level 3 advances early-fluent readers toward fluency through increased text and concept load, less reliance on visuals, longer sentences, and more literary language.

Level 4 builds reading stamina by providing more text per page, increased use of punctuation, greater variation in sentence patterns, and increasingly challenging vocabulary.

Level 5 encourages children to move from "learning to read" to "reading to learn" by providing even more text, varied writing styles, and less familiar topics.

Whichever book is right for your reader, Blastoff! Readers are the perfect books to build confidence and encourage a love of reading that will last a lifetime!

This edition first published in 2020 by Bellwether Media, Inc.

No part of this publication may be reproduced in whole or in part without written permission of the publisher. For information regarding permission, write to Bellwether Media, Inc., Attention: Permissions Department, 6012 Blue Circle Drive, Minnetonka, MN 55343.

Library of Congress Cataloging-in-Publication Data

Names: Moening, Kate, author.
Title: Serena Williams : Tennis Star / by Kate Moening.
Description: Minneapolis, MN : Bellwether Media, Inc., 2020. | Series: Blastoff! Readers : Women Leading the Way |
    Includes bibliographical references and index. | Audience: Ages: 5-8. | Audience: Grades: K-3.
Identifiers: LCCN 2018053546 (print) | LCCN 2019004505 (ebook) | ISBN 9781618916747 (ebook) |
    ISBN 9781644871027 (hardcover : alk. paper) | ISBN 781618917256 (pbk. : alk. paper)
Subjects: LCSH: Williams, Serena, 1981–Juvenile literature. | Tennis players–United States–Biography–Juvenile
    literature. | African American women tennis players–Biography–Juvenile literature.
Classification: LCC GV994.W55 (ebook) | LCC GV994.W55 M66 2020 (print) | DDC 796.342 [B] –dc23
LC record available at https://lccn.loc.gov/2018053546

Editor: Al Albertson   Designer: Andrea Schneider

Printed in the United States of America, North Mankato, MN.

Table of Contents

Who Is Serena Williams?

Serena Williams is a **professional** tennis player.

She is one of the greatest **athletes** who has ever lived!

2015 U.S. Open Championship

"[A] CHAMPION IS DEFINED NOT BY THEIR WINS BUT BY HOW THEY CAN RECOVER WHEN THEY FALL." (2012)

Serena grew up in Compton, California. Her dad taught Serena and her sister, Venus, to play tennis.

Serena with her father and sister

California

Compton

He taught them to imagine themselves as **champions**!

Getting Her Start

Serena was small. But she was strong and smart. She believed in herself and worked very hard at tennis.

When Serena was 14,
she turned professional!

Serena Williams Profile

Birthday: September 26, 1981

Hometown: Compton, California

Industry: sports (tennis)

Education:
- homeschooled
- fashion design classes
  (Art Institute of Fort Lauderdale)

Influences and Heroes:
- Richard Williams (father)
- Oracene Price (mother)
- Venus Williams (sister)
- Billie Jean King (tennis player)

Serena kept getting
better as she grew up.

Serena winning her first Grand Slam in 1999

In 1999, she won her first **Grand Slam**!

Changing the World

Serena winning a gold medal
at the London 2012 Olympics

Serena has won more Grand Slams
than any player since 1973!
She has four **Olympic** gold medals.

There are few
African-American
tennis players. Serena has
played for over 20 years!

Some people treat Serena unfairly because she is an African-American woman. Serena is tough. She knows their actions are wrong.

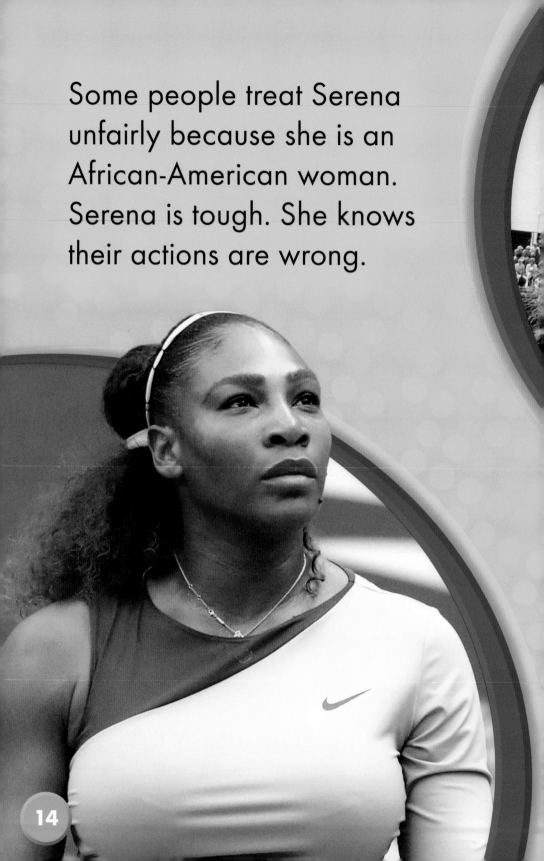

Many people support Serena!
They respect her great work.

Serena uses her fame to help people. She works to help families that are hurt by **violence**.

Serena also started her own clothing **company**!

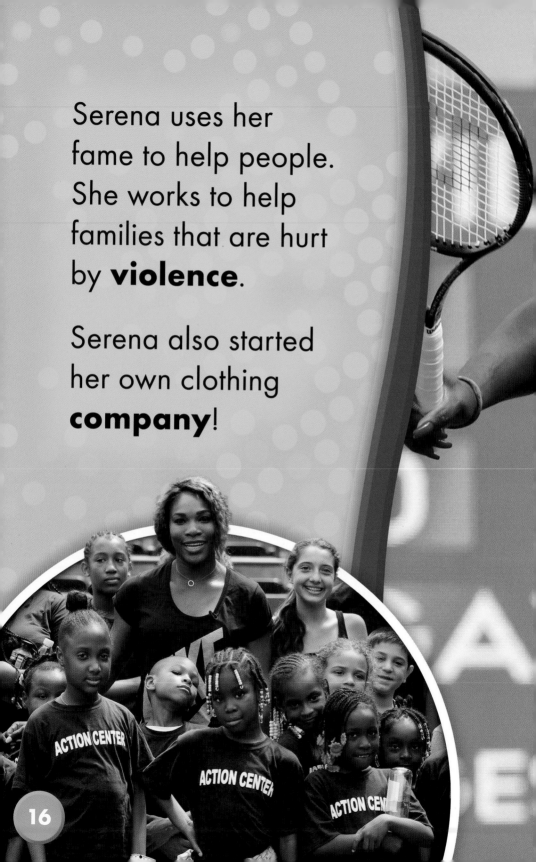

"I HAVE SPENT MANY...HOURS ON THE COURT WORKING FOR MY ONE MOMENT." (2003)

Serena's Future

Serena will keep playing tennis!

Serena Williams Timeline

1995	Serena begins to play tennis as a professional
1999	Serena wins her first Grand Slam
2002-2003	Serena wins all four Grand Slams in a row; people call this the "Serena Slam."
2017	Serena wins her 23rd Grand Slam
2018	Serena starts her clothing company, "Serena"

She wants to win as many Grand Slams as she can.

Serena also wants **equality**. She fights for women and people of color.

Serena wants fair treatment, on and off the court!

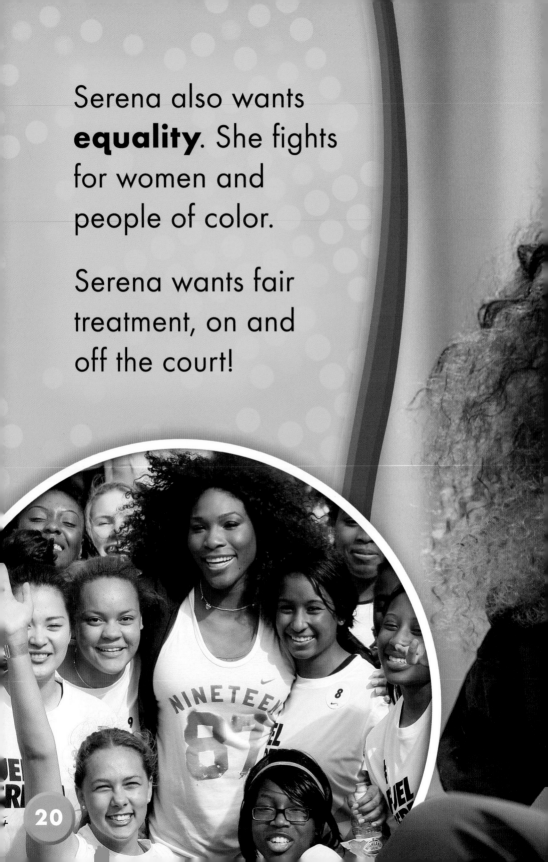

"MAKE SURE YOU'RE VERY COURAGEOUS: BE STRONG, BE EXTREMELY KIND, AND ABOVE ALL BE HUMBLE." (2015)

Glossary

athletes—people who are trained in or good at games that require physical strength and skill

champions—winners of first prize or first place

company—a group that makes, buys, or sells goods for money

equality—just and fair treatment for all groups of people

Grand Slam—one of the four major contests in professional tennis; the Grand Slams are the Australian Open, French Open, Wimbledon, and United States Open.

Olympic—related to the Olympic Games; the Olympic Games are worldwide summer or winter sports contests held in a different country every four years.

professional—paid to participate in a sport or activity

violence—the use of force in a way that harms a person or property

To Learn More

AT THE LIBRARY

Bryant, Howard. *Sisters and Champions: The Story of Venus and Serena Williams*. New York, N.Y.: Philomel Books, 2018.

Cline-Ransome, Lesa. *Game Changers: The Story of Venus and Serena Williams*. New York, N.Y.: Simon & Schuster Books for Young Readers, 2018.

Raum, Elizabeth. *Serena Williams*. Mankato, Minn.: Amicus INK, 2018.

ON THE WEB

FACTSURFER

Factsurfer.com gives you a safe, fun way to find more information.

1. Go to www.factsurfer.com.

2. Enter "Serena Williams" into the search box and click 🔍.

3. Select your book cover to see a list of related web sites.

Index